TURTLE FARMING FOR BEGINNERS

Step-By-Step Guide To Raising Healthy Tortoise, Building The Perfect Habitat, And Maximizing Profits With Low-Cost Methods

Holden bodhi

Contents

CHAPTER ONE 9
  Overview Of Turtle Farming...9
    Recognising The Practice Of Turtle Farming 9
    An Overview Of Turtle Farming 11
    Advantages And Difficulties 14
    Important Words And Definitions 16

CHAPTER TWO...19
  Selecting The Appropriate Turtle Type 19
    Often Used Species In Farming........................19
    Habitat And Care Needs Of The Species 22
    Legal Aspects And Licenses 25

CHAPTER THREE 29
  Establishing The Farm 29
    Choosing An Appropriate Location 29
    Creating Turtle Shelters 31
    Installing Necessary Equipment 33

CHAPTER FOUR..37
  Comprehending Nutrition In Turtles 37
    The Significance Of Balanced Diet 37
    Feeding Plans And Quantities.........................42
    Particular Diets And Supplements 44

CHAPTER FIVE 49
  Medical And Veterinary Services 49
    Typical Diseases Of Turtles..............................49

- Preventive Health Actions 51
- Locating A Veterinarian 53

CHAPTER SIX 57
- Turtle Reproduction 57
  - Breeding Conditions And Methods 57
  - Care For Incubation And Hatchlings 59
  - Controlling The Growth Of Hatchlings 62

CHAPTER SEVEN 65
- Taking Care Of Turtle Environment 65
  - Overview Of Turtle Environments 65
  - Water Purity And Filtration 67
  - Lighting And Temperature 68
  - Enhancement Of Habitat 70

CHAPTER EIGHT 73
- Daily Upkeep And Repair 73
  - Standard Cleaning Techniques 73
  - Keeping An Eye On Turtle Behaviour 75
  - Maintaining And Managing Records 78

CHAPITRE NINE 81
- Promoting And Getting Rid Of Turtles 81
  - Recognising The Market 81
  - Strategies For Pricing 84
  - Channels Of Sales And Customer Engagement 87

Chapter Ten 91

A Legal And Ethical Perspective 91
    Rules And Adherence 91
    Ethical Methods In Agriculture 94
    Impact On The Environment 96
CHAPTER ELEVEN 101
    Developing And Growing Your Farm 101
    Developing Infrastructure 101
    Employing And Educating Personnel 104
    Planning Your Finances For Growth 107
    Conclusin 113

Copyright © 2024 by Holden bodhi

All rights reserved.

No part of this publication may be reproduced, distributed, or transmitted in any form or by any means, including photocopying, recording, or other electronic or mechanical methods, without the prior written permission of the publisher, except in the case of brief quotations embodied in critical reviews and certain other non commercial uses permitted by copyright law.

DISCLAIMER

The information provided in this book, is intended for educational and informational purposes only. The content is based on research, personal experiences, and general knowledge about farming. It is not intended to substitute professional advice or expert consultation. Readers are encouraged to seek professional guidance when implementing any practices or techniques discussed in this book.

The author and publisher make no representations or warranties of any kind regarding the accuracy, applicability, or completeness of the contents of this book. Any reliance you place on such information is strictly at your own risk. The author and publisher shall not be held liable for any damages, losses, or injuries resulting from the use of the information provided.

Additionally, the author does not endorse, recommend, or affiliate with any individual, product, service, website, organization, or brand mentioned or referenced in this book. Any such references are solely for informational purposes, and no warranty or guarantee is implied. The inclusion of these references does not imply any endorsement or partnership by the author.

By reading this book, you acknowledge and accept that the author and publisher are not responsible for any consequences arising from your use of the information provided.

CHAPTER ONE

Overview Of Turtle Farming

Recognising The Practice Of Turtle Farming

The raising and care of turtles for a variety of objectives, such as commercial production, conservation, and scientific study, is known as "turtle farming." Small-scale businesses with a few tanks to large-scale farms with substantial infrastructure can engage in this technique.

A combination of husbandry techniques, biological knowledge, and the right tools are needed for turtle farming Establishing an environment that promotes turtles' growth and health while controlling their reproduction and general well-being is the main objective of turtle farming.

The Value of Farming Turtles

Turtle farming is important to the commercial and conservation sectors. It offers a regulated habitat for the raising of turtles, which can lessen the strain on wild populations and aid in the preservation of species. It also helps local economies in some areas by supplying markets with turtle meat, shells, and other goods. Anyone wishing to establish or run a successful turtle farm must have a solid understanding of the principles of the industry.

Principal Aims of Turtle Farming

Ensuring the welfare of the turtles, maximising development rates, and accomplishing successful reproduction are the main goals of turtle farming. Ethical norms and environmental requirements must also be followed by farms. A thorough understanding of turtle biology and appropriate management techniques are necessary to achieve these goals and keep the operation sustainable.

Getting Started with Turtle Farming

Careful preparation and study must be done before establishing a turtle farm. This entails choosing the proper kind of turtle, comprehending the requirements of their habitat, and making the necessary equipment purchases. Furthermore, understanding regional laws and consumer preferences will assist guide your farming endeavour. A profitable turtle farming enterprise will be built from the ground up with a well-defined plan and attainable objectives.

An Overview Of Turtle Farming
Systems Used in Turtle Farming

Systems for raising turtles might differ greatly depending on the size of the farm and its objectives. Turtles are raised in tanks or ponds in aquaculture-based settings, and land-based enclosures are used in terrestrial systems. Each system has benefits and drawbacks, and the decision will be influenced by things like the type of turtles being farmed, the amount of money available, and the available space.

Turtle species used in farming

Turtles can be farmed in a variety of species, each with specific needs and market value. For example, species with high demand and adaptability, such Painted Turtles and Red-Eared Sliders, are common in commercial farms. On the other hand, farms may raise endangered species mainly for conservation. Comprehending the distinct requirements and attributes of every species is vital for prosperous farming.

Using efficient farm management techniques is crucial to keeping a turtle farm fruitful and healthy.

This entails controlling the temperature, keeping the water clean, and making sure the turtles are getting enough food. Other crucial facets of farm management include routine health examinations and illness control. By putting these procedures into place, you may contribute to the farm's prosperity and the welfare of the turtles.

Environmental and Regulatory Aspects

Environmental concerns and a number of restrictions apply to turtle farming. To conduct business lawfully and morally, compliance with national and international laws is required.

This entails following regulations pertaining to conservation, habitat management, and animal care. Comprehending and using these guidelines aids in averting legal complications and advances environmentally friendly agricultural methods.

Advantages And Difficulties
Advantages of Raising Turtles

There are several advantages to turtle farming, such as the possibility of financial gain, support for conservation efforts, and educational opportunities. Economically, selling turtles, their eggs, and other goods can generate a consistent revenue through turtle farming. Furthermore, by easing the strain on wild species and offering a controlled setting for breeding and research, farming can support conservation efforts. Turtle farms can be excellent educational resources for learning about the biology and conservation of turtles.

Difficulties Associated with Turtle Farming

There are drawbacks to turtle farming despite its advantages. These include handling the various requirements that various turtle species have, preventing any illnesses, and making sure that farming methods are sustainable. A substantial financial commitment is also needed for infrastructure, equipment, and continuing upkeep in turtle farming. Effectively addressing these issues is essential to the farm's long-term success.

Goals for the Environment and Economy in Balance

A primary obstacle in the practice of turtle farming is striking a balance between financial objectives and ecological and moral issues. Turtle farms have to balance making a profit with protecting the health of their animals and reducing their environmental effect.

entails putting into practice sustainable methods, such cutting back on waste and saving resources, in order to preserve a balance between environmental responsibility and economic success.

Prospects for Turtle Farming in the Future

With the development of technology and growing public awareness of the need for conservation, the future of turtle farming seems bright. Farms can become more sustainable and efficient through new farming techniques and better turtle care. Furthermore, the growing demand for ethical and sustainable food sources could spur additional growth in the turtle farming sector. In order to maintain their competitiveness and support the industry's good growth, farmers should embrace new technologies and stay up to date on industry trends.

Important Words And Definitions
Important Terms for Turtle Farming

Anyone working in turtle farming needs to be familiar with important terminology and definitions. Among the crucial terms are:

• Aquaculture: The controlled environment rearing of aquatic species, such as turtles.

• Husbandry: the raising, rearing, and caring of animals.

• Incubation: Maintaining the proper temperature and humidity levels for turtle eggs to facilitate a successful hatch.

• Biosecurity: Taking precautions to stop infections from entering and spreading among farm animals.

Terms Used in Turtle Farming Glossary

Turtles' upper shell is called a carapace.

Turtles' lower shell is called a plactron.

• Terrarium: Turtles are housed in enclosed spaces made of glass or plastic.

• Herpetology: The study of amphibians and reptiles.

Comprehending the Anatomy and Physiology of Turtles

An understanding of the anatomy and physiology of turtles is essential for successful rearing. Understanding the roles played by the many organ systems, the fundamental requirements for preserving health, and the composition and operation of the plastron and carapace are important. Understanding these factors facilitates controlling health issues and delivering the proper care.

Typical Farm Acronyms

- Turtle Farming Operations, or TFO.

- Turtle Population Management, or TPM.

- Aquatic Wildlife Welfare, or AWW.

In order to facilitate communication within the business and to refer to particular facets of turtle farming, these acronyms are frequently utilised.

CHAPTER TWO

Selecting The Appropriate Turtle Type

Often Used Species In Farming

The right species must be chosen before starting a turtle farming operation to ensure success. There are several species of turtles that are good for farming; each has its own requirements and traits. Here, we'll examine a few well-known species of turtles that are frequently raised and offer advice on which ones are good for novices.

1. The Trachemys scripta elegans, or red-eared slider

A popular species for farming because of its versatility and low maintenance requirements is the Red-Eared Slider. This species can survive in both freshwater ponds and aquariums and is easily identified by its red ear patterns. Red-eared sliders can reach a length of 12 inches and are renowned for their strong health. To be healthy, they need a UV-lit basking area and a large enough water environment in which to swim and feed.

2. Turtle with Paint (Chrysemys picta)

For novices, the Painted Turtle is still another fantastic option. This species, which is native to North America, is distinguished by the vivid colours and patterns of its shell and can adapt to a variety of aquatic conditions. Painted Turtles usually reach a length of 6 to 8 inches, making them smaller than Red-Eared Sliders. Shallow water with lots of greenery and places to sunbathe is what they want. Small fish, insects, and water plants make up the majority of their diet.

3. Chelydra serpentina, the common snapping turtle

The Common Snapping Turtle is a good choice for anyone seeking a species that is more hardy and durable. This species is renowned for having strong jaws and an aggressive attitude. Snapping Turtles are usually raised in large, enclosed ponds or tanks and can reach a maximum length of 18 inches. Being omnivores, they consume a wide range of aquatic life, such as insects, fish, and amphibians. Their temperament and stature necessitate extra attention and safe environments.

4. The Centrochelys sulcata tortoise

The African Spurred Tortoise, or Sulcata Tortoise, is a terrestrial species that is becoming more and more popular in turtle farming. One of the largest species of tortoises, individuals can grow up to 30 inches in length. Sulcata tortoises need lots of room to wander around in a dry, arid habitat. As herbivores, they consume vegetables, hay, and grasses. Due to their large size and lengthy lifespan, they require a substantial habitat and maintenance budget.

5. (Terrapene carolina carolina) Eastern Box Turtle

The semi-terrestrial Eastern Box Turtle is a popular choice because to its distinct look and small stature. They can reach a length of 6 to 8 inches and have a unique domed shell. The habitats that box turtles can adapt to include gardens and wooded regions. Their food consists of a variety of fruits, vegetables, and insects. They work well in backyard farming setups because of their modest size and natural behaviour.

Habitat And Care Needs Of The Species

For the wellbeing and productivity of each species of turtle, certain habitat and care needs must be satisfied. For turtle farming to be effective, it is imperative that these demands are understood.

1. Habitat and Care of the Red-Eared Slider

A clean, well-kept aquatic habitat with spaces for swimming and basking is necessary for red-eared sliders. A UV-lit basking platform and a filtration system should be included in the aquatic habitat to maintain clean water. The ideal water temperature range is 75–80°F, whereas the ideal basking area is a little warmer. To stop sickness, regular water changes and observation are required.

2. Care and Habitat for Painted Turtles

Shallow water with lots of plants is ideal for painted turtles to flourish. To support their natural foraging and basking habits, their habitat should have both shallow and deeper areas. For the purpose of encouraging healthy shell growth and preventing metabolic bone disease, they need a basking place with UV light. To avoid health problems, the water should be kept between 70 and 75°F, and the surroundings should be kept clean.

3. Standard Snapping Turtle Habitat and Maintenance

Given their size and habits, common snapping turtles require a big, enclosed pond or tank. There should be plenty of hiding places and places to bask as well as deep and shallow sections in the habitat. Because they are more violent, snapping turtles need to be kept in safe enclosures to avoid harm or escape. They should eat a variety of meals, such as premium commercial foods and live prey.

4. habitat and care of the Sulcata tortoise

A large, dry enclosure that closely resembles the native desert environment of Sulcata tortoises is required. Sand and soil mixtures are good substrate options for the enclosure that facilitate burrowing. To shield them from harsh weather, they need to have access to a heated shelter. For their health, they require a diet high in grasses and hay as well as regular access to sunshine. Regular veterinary treatment is also necessary for Sulcata Tortoises to maintain their health.

5. Habitat and Care of Eastern Box Turtles

Semi-terrestrial environments with a balance of sunny and shaded spots are ideal for Eastern Box Turtles. There should be a range of plants and digging spaces within their enclosure. It is essential to have access to shallow water for bathing and drinking. Box turtles need a diverse diet, and extra calcium and vitamins can be beneficial. To protect them from illness and to maintain their general health, their habitat needs to be maintained clean.

Legal Aspects And Licenses

Getting the required permits and being aware of the legal ramifications are essential before beginning turtle farming. Regulations pertaining to the ownership and farming of turtles vary by location. Below is a summary of the important legal factors to think about.

1. Licenses and Permits

The majority of places want licenses or permits in order to farm turtles, particularly if you want to raise species that are protected or endangered. To find out the exact rules in your area, it is imperative that you contact the environmental and wildlife agencies in your community. Turtle collection, breeding, and sales may be subject to permits.

2. Regulations Specific to Species

Depending on their level of conservation, certain species of turtles may be subject to special rules. Special permissions and tougher criteria are frequently needed for endangered species. To make sure you are in compliance with all legal requirements, be sure to investigate the particular legislation pertaining to the species you intend to farm.

3. Assessments of the Environmental Impact

Before establishing a turtle farm, you might need to perform an environmental impact study in specific areas. The possible impacts of your farming operations on nearby ecosystems and wildlife are assessed by this assessment. It makes sure that the farming methods you use don't harm the environment.

4. Maintaining Documents and Reports

There are numerous governments that demand thorough reporting and record-keeping of turtle farming operations.

This covers the recording of sales, breeding, and health care. Precise records are essential for audits and inspections as well as for proving compliance with legislation.

5. Standards for Animal Welfare

In turtle farming, adherence to standards for animal welfare is crucial. Guidelines for the humane care of turtles, including as appropriate housing, diet, and medical attention, may be included in regulations. Making sure your turtles are healthy not only satisfies legal obligations but also supports a profitable and moral farming enterprise.

CHAPTER THREE

Establishing The Farm

Choosing An Appropriate Location

Selecting the ideal site is the first and most important stage in starting a turtle farm. This choice affects not just the growth and well-being of your turtles but also the farm's overall productivity. When choosing a site, a number of things should be taken into account.

1. environment & Temperature: Because turtles are extremely sensitive to temperature fluctuations, it's critical to choose a site with a stable environment. To prevent sharp variations in temperature, the area should ideally have a moderate climate. If the winters are harsh where you live, you might want to think about installing inside enclosures or heating systems to keep the temperature at a comfortable level.

2. Closeness to Water Sources: Turtles need clean water for bathing and drinking. As a result, the location you have chosen should be close to a dependable water source, like a lake, river, or well. The health of your turtles can be negatively impacted by pollution and toxins, so make sure the water source is free of them.

3. Soil and Drainage: Building turtle enclosures and keeping them clean require appropriate soil conditions. Proper drainage of the soil is necessary to avoid waterlogging, which can cause health problems. To make sure the soil is suitable for building enclosures and keeping a clean environment, test it.

4. Infrastructure and accessibility: It should be simple to get to your farm for maintenance and transportation needs. Examine the current infrastructure, such as the utilities, trash disposal systems, and roadways. A location with good connections will help your farm run

more smoothly and simplify logistics management.

5. Zoning and Regulations: Research your community's zoning laws and rules pertaining to farming and raising animals. To prevent any legal problems, make sure the location is compliant with these rules. Prior to starting operations, obtain any licenses or permits that are required.

Creating Turtle Shelters

Careful planning is necessary when designing turtle enclosures to provide your turtles with a secure and comfortable living space. A well-thought-out cage reduces stress and encourages healthy growth. These are the main things to think about:

1. Size and Space of Enclosure: The enclosure's dimensions are determined by the quantity and kind of turtles you intend to raise. Every turtle needs enough room to walk about,

sunbathe and swim. Larger cages are generally easier to maintain over time and offer better living circumstances for turtles.

2. Features of the Habitat: It is essential for turtles' welfare to replicate their native habitat. Incorporate elements like hiding places, water zones, and basking regions. Platforms or logs can be used to create basking places, and water zones need to be deep enough for swimming and cleaning.

3. Temperature Control: The health of the turtles depends on the enclosure's proper temperature being maintained. Install air conditioning or heating units as needed to control the temperature. Furthermore, make sure the temperature stays within the optimal range for your kind of turtle by using thermostats to monitor and regulate it.

4. illumination: For turtles to survive, there must be adequate illumination. Offer artificial and

natural lighting to replicate the day-night cycle. Turtles need UVB light in order to make vitamin D3 and keep their shells healthy. Make sure the lighting arrangement is positioned appropriately to prevent glare and offer uniform illumination.

5. Safety and Security: It's crucial to keep your turtles safe from harm and to allow them to escape. To keep outside animals out, erect strong fences and barriers. Examine the enclosure frequently for indications of wear and tear or vulnerabilities, and take immediate action to fix them.

Installing Necessary Equipment

A healthy and productive turtle farm depends on installing the proper equipment. The apparatus guarantees that your turtles will always have access to fresh water, suitable lighting, and a secure habitat. The following is a list of all the necessary supplies for your turtle farm:

1. Filtration Systems: Investing in a high-quality filtration system is crucial since clean water is critical for turtle health. Select a filter that can efficiently remove contaminants from the water in your enclosure while handling its volume. To guarantee the filter operates at its best, clean and maintain it on a regular basis.

2. Heating and Cooling Systems: Install heating and cooling systems as necessary to control the enclosure's temperature. While fans or air conditioners can provide cooling during hot weather, heating pads, lamps, and heaters can assist maintain warmth. Make sure the systems work with the size and design of your enclosure.

3. Lighting Systems: To give your turtles the light they require, install UVB and heat lamps. Heat lamps mimic natural sunlight and give warmth; UVB lights are essential for calcium metabolism and shell health. To prevent overheating or inadequate lighting, place the

lamps at the proper height and distance from one another.

4. Water Quality Testing Kits: In order to avoid health problems, it is imperative to regularly test the quality of the water. Purchase testing kits for water quality to measure things like ammonia, nitrites, nitrates, and pH. You can avoid the accumulation of dangerous materials and maintain ideal water conditions with the aid of routine testing.

5. Tools for Cleaning and Feeding: Outfit your farm with cleaning and feeding equipment. Feeding tools could be easy-to-clean and refill feeders or specialised dishes. Cleaning supplies like nets, brushes, and scoops will enable you to keep your turtles' habitat tidy and sanitary.

Your turtle farm can have a healthy atmosphere if you carefully choose a good location, build efficient cages, and install necessary equipment. These actions are essential to guaranteeing both the general health and success of your turtle farming endeavour as well as the wellbeing of your turtles.

CHAPTER FOUR

Comprehending Nutrition In Turtles

The Significance Of Balanced Diet

Turtles are unusual animals with distinct food requirements that change according to their species, age, and environment. For turtles to stay healthy and long in life, it is essential to understand their diet. In order to sustain development, reproduction, and general well-being, turtles need the correct combination of vitamins, minerals, proteins, fats, and carbs, which can only be provided through proper diet.

A healthy diet that is well-balanced supports a turtle's strong immune system, healthy shell, and healthy organ function. Inadequate dietary intake can result in multiple health complications, including as digestive disorders, malformations of the shell, and metabolic bone disease. Therefore, it's critical to supply a diet specific to each type of turtle.

The Nutritious Needs of Various Species

Every kind of turtle has distinct nutritional requirements. For instance, whereas terrestrial turtles would need more fibre and veggies in their diet, aquatic turtles often need a diet higher in protein. It's critical to comprehend the particular nutritional requirements of the turtles you are raising in order to guarantee their success.

For example, because they are omnivores, box turtles require a diet rich in both plant and animal materials, such as worms, insects, and leafy greens. In contrast, tortoises eat a diet high in grasses, leaves, and vegetables because they are mostly herbivores. Developing the right diet will be aided by researching the unique nutritional needs of each species.

Essential Elements of a Turtle Diet

Typically, a balanced turtle diet consists of:

• Proteins: necessary for development and repair. found in fish, insects, and prepared turtle food.

• Fats: Promote cell activity and supply energy. included in several commercial feeds and fish oils.

• Carbohydrates: Provide energy and facilitate digestion. present in several cereals, fruits, and vegetables.

Minerals and vitamins are essential for metabolic processes. Calcium, vitamin D, and vitamin A are very crucial for the health of shells.

A diverse range of these ingredients guarantees that turtles eat a diet that is health-promoting and well-rounded.

Types of Food for Turtles

Trade-Sector Turtle Foods

The dietary requirements of various turtle species are taken into account while creating commercial turtle meals. Pellets, sticks, and freeze-dried alternatives are among them. Selecting premium commercial food guarantees that turtles will have a good variety of nutrients.

Pellets are a popular choice for a main course. For different species and ages, they are available in a range of sizes and formulas. Pellets are easy to prepare and provide a well-balanced combination of lipids, proteins, and other nutrients.

Sticks: Used for larger turtles, sticks are comparable to pellets. Depending on the habitat of the species, they can either float or sink.

Foods that have been freeze-dried are easy to preserve and provide a rich source of protein. Rather than being the main source of nutrition, they are frequently utilised as supplements or treats.

Organic Foods

Apart from commercial meals, a range of natural foods can be beneficial for turtles.

Eat live or frozen fish, worms, and insects, according to aquatic turtles. These foods give important fats and proteins and replicate their natural diet.

Leafy greens, fruits, and a range of fresh vegetables are beneficial for terrestrial turtles. Certain species also eat insects or fried eggs as tiny sources of protein.

DIY Diets

To guarantee the freshness and quality of the food, some turtle farmers choose to make their own meals. Diets manufactured at home can be tailored to your turtles' individual requirements.

Recipes: Finely diced fruits and vegetables, as well as protein sources combined with supplements, can be found in homemade diets.

It's critical to look for and adhere to recipes that offer a nutritional profile that is balanced.

Preparation and Storage: To avoid contamination, make sure homemade diets are prepared in a hygienic setting and stored appropriately. Every day or as needed, fresh food should be made, and any leftovers should be taken out of the habitat right away.

Feeding Plans And Quantities
Creating a Schedule for Feeding

To keep farmed turtles healthy, a well-planned feeding program is essential. The species, age, and size of the turtles determine how often and how much they eat.

Juvenile Turtles: These animals typically need to be fed more frequently—two or three times a day. For their bodies to continue developing, they require a steady stream of nutrients.

Adult turtles: Usually fed once a day or every other day, but they can be fed less frequently. Taking into account the turtle's size and activity level, the amount of food should be modified.

How Much Food Is?

The amount of food given to each turtle should be customised to meet its unique demands. Underfeeding can result in malnutrition, while overfeeding can cause obesity and other health problems.

Portion Sizes: Generally speaking, a turtle should receive between one and two percent of its body weight in food. Depending on the turtle's activity level and growth pace, this can be changed.

Observation: Keep a regular eye on the turtles' weight and modify the feeding portions as necessary. If changes are required, it can also be determined by keeping an eye on their behaviour and health.

Particulars Regarding Feeding

Certain turtles may require a particular diet because of age or medical issues.

Turtles that are breeding or pregnant may need more nourishment to sustain their offspring. You might need to take more calcium and protein.

Turtles that are ill or injured may require a changed diet to help them heal. For specialised dietary advice, speaking with a veterinarian is recommended.

Seasonal Adjustments: Depending on the season, some turtles may require different diets. Certain animals, for example, can consume less in the winter and more in the summer.

Particular Diets And Supplements
Different Supplement Types

Supplements can guarantee that turtles get all the vital vitamins and minerals they require and help close nutritional deficits.

Supplemental calcium is essential for the growth of shells and general bone health. obtainable as a liquid or powder, and it need to be often incorporated into the diet.

Vitamin supplements: Particularly crucial for turtles whose diets aren't very diverse. Supplements containing vitamins A and D are widely utilised.

Probiotics: Can enhance nutrition absorption and promote intestinal health. They can be served separately or as an addition to the diet.

Personalised Diets for Particular Needs

Depending on their condition, age, or species-specific requirements, some turtles might need to eat particular diets.

High-protein diets are necessary for turtle growth or reproduction. You can use high-quality sources of protein, such as seafood or speciality commercial foods.

Diets low in protein: Good for elderly turtles or turtles who are prone to obesity. Give priority to low-fat, high-fiber foods.

Hydration Requirements: Some turtle species, especially those that live in water, need extra water sources. It is crucial to always have access to fresh, clean water.

Observation and Modifications

Turtle diet and supplement adjustments will be aided by routinely evaluating the health and condition of the animals.

Health Checks: Routine medical examinations can determine whether dietary changes are necessary. This involves keeping an eye on the weight, general activity levels, and shell condition.

Consultation with Experts: A veterinarian or a turtle nutrition specialist can offer specialised advise and solutions for complicated food requirements or health concerns.

CHAPTER FIVE

Medical And Veterinary Services

Typical Diseases Of Turtles
Overview of Turtle Illnesses

Like any other animal, turtles can get a variety of illnesses. It is essential to comprehend these prevalent ailments in order to guarantee the health of your turtles. Turtles can get physical wounds, parasite infestations, bacterial and viral diseases, and more.

infections of the respiratory system

Turtles frequently get respiratory infections, which are frequently brought on by unfavourable environmental factors like low temperatures or inadequate ventilation. Breathing difficulties, nasal discharge, and fatigue are among the symptoms. If left untreated, chronic respiratory infections might result in more serious health problems.

Rotten Shell

A fungal or bacterial condition known as "shell rot" causes the turtle's shell to become fragile, discoloured, and in extreme situations, to start losing portions of it. Injuries to the shell or unhygienic conditions in the habitat frequently lead to the infection. Preventative measures include keeping the habitat clean and doing routine inspections.

Insect parasites

A turtle's health can be impacted by both internal and external parasites, such as worms and ticks and mites. Unusual shedding, skin-visible parasites, or faecal alterations are possible symptoms. Depending on the type of parasite, treatment typically consists of topical treatments or deworming drugs.

Egg Attachment

Egg binding, a condition in which eggs become stuck inside the body, can be uncomfortable and could lead to health issues for female turtles. To treat this problem, a veterinarian must act right away.

fungus-related infections

Skin and shell infections are among the bodily areas of a turtle that can be impacted by fungi. Patches of aberrant growth or colouring are what define them. Medications with antifungal properties and bettering the turtle's living environment are common forms of treatment.

Preventive Health Actions

Keeping the Ideal Habitat Conditions

Ensuring turtles live in an ideal habitat is one of the best methods to prevent health problems in them. This entails offering suitable humidity ranges, illumination levels, and temperature ranges. An environment that is kept up helps ward against illnesses and ailments brought on by stress.

Continual Sanitation and Personal Care

To avoid infections and illnesses, the turtle's habitat must be cleaned on a regular basis. This include emptying the waste from the tank, cleaning it, and making sure the water is filtered and replaced on a regular basis. Maintaining good hygiene stops dangerous fungus and germs from growing.

Well-Balanced Diet

You must feed your turtles a balanced diet if you want them to be healthy overall. Make sure their diet has the right proportion of veggies, proteins, and other nutrients. To make sure they get all the nutrients they need, try not to overfeed them and offer a variety of meals.

Continual Health Examinations

For the early identification of any potential health risks, routine health examinations are essential. You can spot issues in your turtles before they get out of hand by keeping an eye out for changes in their behaviour, appetite, or physical appearance.

Shots and Add-ons

Turtles don't usually need immunisations, but keeping them healthy can benefit from taking certain vitamins. For example, calcium supplements are crucial for the general health and well-being of shells. To find out if your turtles need vitamins, speak with a veterinarian.

Locating A Veterinarian

The Value of Expertise

Selecting a veterinarian with expertise in caring for reptiles is essential for the wellbeing of your turtle. Veterinarians that specialise in reptiles are qualified to handle the particular health problems that turtles encounter and may offer expert treatment and guidance.

Studies and Suggestions

Look up local vets who practice reptile medicine first. Advice from local reptile clubs or other turtle owners can be quite helpful. To determine the veterinarian practice's repute, look for reviews and testimonials.

First Consultation

Arrange a consultation to evaluate the veterinarian's methods and facilities. Talk about your turtle's individual requirements and any health issues at this visit. A competent veterinarian will do a comprehensive checkup and offer clear guidance on maintenance and treatment.

Access to and Care for Emergencies

Make sure the veterinarian you select provides emergency care. Turtles sometimes have health problems that need to be attended to right away, therefore it's critical for you to have a trustworthy emergency contact for your turtle.

Establishing a Bond

For continued care, building a strong rapport with your veterinarian is advantageous. Keeping your turtle healthy and taking care of any problems that may come up is facilitated by routine visits and honest communication. During appointments, provide your veterinarian with comprehensive documents on your turtle's condition and medical interventions.

CHAPTER SIX

Turtle Reproduction

Breeding Conditions And Methods

Overview of Breeding Turtles

The careful process of breeding turtles necessitates a deep comprehension of the unique requirements and innate behaviours of the species. Replicating their native habitat as nearly as possible and providing the right care and conditions are essential to the successful reproduction of turtles.

Choosing Breeding Stock

Selecting quality breeding stock is essential. It is best to choose mature, healthy turtles that show no symptoms of illness or abnormalities. It's critical to comprehend turtle sexual dimorphism, as males and females frequently differ morphologically. For instance, the concave plastron of several species' males helps them mount the female during mating.

Establishing the Ideal Setting

Replicating the natural habitat of the turtles is necessary to provide an ideal breeding environment. This entails supplying enough room, keeping the pH and temperature of the water at the proper levels, and more. Replicating these environmental characteristics as closely as possible can increase the likelihood of successful breeding, as turtles frequently reproduce in specific settings.

surroundings

For turtles to breed, temperature is essential. For the majority of turtle species, reproductive behaviour is stimulated within a particular temperature range. In order to control the turtles' reproductive cycles, light cycles should also replicate natural day and night cycles. Since female turtles require a secure location to deposit their eggs, providing proper nesting places is also crucial.

Observation and Modifications

It is essential to regularly observe the health and behaviour of the turtles. Making the required modifications can be aided by keeping an eye on mating behaviours and making sure the breeding season's conditions stay stable. Prompt attention to any indication of stress or illness is necessary to prevent any negative impact on the breeding process.

Care For Incubation And Hatchlings

Fundamentals of Incubation

The crucial period that follows the female turtle laying her eggs is called incubation. Controlling the humidity and temperature during incubation is necessary to guarantee that the eggs develop as intended. The needs for incubation vary throughout turtle species, so it's critical to adhere to species-specific protocols.

Configuring the Environment for Incubation

The conditions of incubation need to be closely monitored. It is crucial to have an incubator that keeps its temperature and humidity levels constant. The optimal temperature range for incubation for the majority of turtle species is 77°F to 82°F (25°C to 28°C). Maintaining a high level of humidity will keep the eggs from drying out.

Managing Eggs

Turtle eggs need to be handled carefully. It is important to carefully transfer the eggs into the incubator while maintaining their orientation. Generally speaking, turning the eggs is not advised unless the rules for that particular species specify otherwise.

Care for Hatchlings

After the eggs hatch, the young must be closely watched. Because they are frequently quite sensitive, hatchlings need a regulated environment in order to survive. Maintaining ideal levels of water temperature and quality is crucial. Since hatchlings are susceptible to illnesses and diseases, it is imperative to provide a clean and healthy environment for them.

Nutrition and Well-Being

For growth and development, hatchlings require a balanced diet. A diet suitable for their species, which usually consists of small, easily digested food, should be supplied to them. They need to have regular health examinations to make sure they are developing normally and to spot any possible problems early.

Moving Hatchlings

Hatchlings may need to be moved to bigger enclosures as they get bigger. For these new habitats to continue growing and developing, it is imperative that they be kept secure and well-maintained. Stress levels will drop and healthy development will be encouraged with proper acclimatisation to their new surroundings.

Controlling The Growth Of Hatchlings
Stages of Growth

Effective handling of turtle hatchlings requires an understanding of their growth stages. Hatchlings go through multiple growth stages, and each one calls for a unique set of circumstances and care. Keeping an eye on their growth and development guarantees that they get the care they require at every stage.

Nutrition and Feeding

A balanced diet is necessary to promote healthy growth. A meal high in nutrients is necessary for hatchlings to sustain their rapid development. This often consists of a combination of minerals, vitamins, and proteins. Their health and optimal growth are supported by regular feeding regimens and nutritional intake monitoring.

Adjustments to Habitat

Hatchlings' habitat requirements will vary as they grow. They will have a habitat that is conducive to their growth if the temperature, water depth, and enclosure size are regularly adjusted. Keeping an eye on their health and behaviour can give you hints about when adjustments are needed.

Health Surveillance

Monitoring hatchling growth requires routine health examinations. Frequent exams aid in the early identification of any possible illnesses, including infections or parasites. Maintaining thorough records of every hatchling's development and health can help spot patterns and quickly address issues.

Getting Ready for the Shift

Managing the growth of hatchlings involves preparing them for the move to a permanent habitat. Reducing stress and encouraging healthy development can be achieved by making sure the new environment satisfies all of their needs and easing them into this new area gradually.

Extended-Duration Care

Planning for the turtles' future requirements as they develop is a crucial part of long-term care. This covers continuing nutrition modifications, habitat management, and health tracking. It is ensured that they develop into adult turtles who are healthy and thriving if they receive consistent and proper care throughout their development.

CHAPTER SEVEN

Taking Care Of Turtle Environment

Overview Of Turtle Environments

Effective habitat management is essential to the health and welfare of your turtles. A well-planned habitat guarantees the health and well-being of your turtles while also imitating their natural surroundings. The basic elements of habitat management are covered in this part, along with habitat design, space needs, and environmental factors.

Creating the Habitat

It's important to comprehend your turtles' native habitat and try to replicate it as much as you can in order to create the ideal home for them. There should be plenty of room for movement, places to sunbathe and access to both land and water in the habitat. Terrestrial turtles need room to wander and feed, whereas aquatic turtles require a body of water big enough for them to swim in.

Space Needs

The kind of turtle you are farming will determine how big the habitat needs to be. Larger species usually need more area. It's generally recommended to provide aquatic turtles with at least 10 gallons of water for every inch of shell length. Large enclosures that enable unrestricted movement and the display of their natural behaviours are necessary for terrestrial turtles.

Environmental Aspects to Take into Account

Maintaining a clean, safe, and humid environment is another aspect of proper habitat management. Hazards such as poisonous plants or sharp objects should not exist within the enclosure. To stop illness and keep the quality of the water high, regular cleaning and maintenance are required.

Water Purity And Filtration

Water Quality Is Important

Aquatic turtle health is largely dependent on the quality of the water. Respiratory infections and shell rot are two health problems that can be brought on by poor water quality. Turtles in their natural habitat will continue to be healthy and content as long as the water is kept clean and in equilibrium.

Systems of Filtration

Sustaining water quality requires effective filtering. Turtle habitats can benefit from a variety of filtration devices, such as chemical, biological, and mechanical filters. While biological filters encourage the growth of helpful microorganisms that break down waste, mechanical filters remove trash and particulates from the water. Toxins and pollutants are partially eliminated by chemical filters.

Testing and Upkeep of Water

Water parameters must be tested frequently to make sure they stay within allowable bounds. Tests for pH, ammonia, nitrite, and nitrate levels are frequently performed. To stop the accumulation of dangerous materials, monitor these factors and change the water regularly.

Controlling Water Temperature

For turtles to remain healthy, the water must be kept at the proper temperature. For the most part, turtle species have a preferred range of temperatures. To keep the water temperature steady and within the intended range, use thermometers and heaters to monitor and control the temperature.

Lighting And Temperature

Control of Temperature

Because they depend on outside heat sources to control their body temperature, turtles are ectothermic. Turtles may successfully thermoregulate when their habitat has a temperature gradient. This entails dividing the cage into warmer and colder zones.

Warming Systems

A variety of heating options are available, such as basking bulbs, under-tank heaters, and heat lamps. The choice of heater relies on the particular requirements of your turtle species, since each type offers pros and cons. Direct heat is typically provided by heat lamps, but a more subdued heat source is provided via under-tank heaters.

Lighting Requirements

For your turtles' general health, proper illumination is crucial. The production of vitamin D3, which aids in the absorption of calcium and maintains the health of the shell, depends on UVB rays. As the UVB intensity gradually drops, provide a light source that covers the entire habitat and replace it on a regular basis.

Cycles of Light

For turtles to replicate natural conditions, there must be a constant cycle of light and shade. Generally speaking, a 12-hour light and 12-hour dark cycle is advised. This encourages healthy habits like feeding and reproducing while assisting in the regulation of the turtles' biological rhythms.

Enhancement Of Habitat
The objective of habitat enhancement

The purpose of enrichment is to encourage your turtles' natural behaviours and enhance their general wellbeing. It offers a variety of sensory and bodily stimulation, which helps ward off boredom and tension.

Different Enrichment Types

There are three categories of enrichment: social, sensory, and physical. Physically stimulating elements include plants, logs, and rocks that promote climbing and exploring. Items that appeal to the turtles' senses, like different textures and smells, are referred to as sensory enrichment. Interactions with other turtles or, if suitable, with animals of different species can be a part of social enrichment.

putting enhancement into practice

Take into account the requirements and preferences of your kind of turtle when enhancing the habitat. Include hiding places, floating platforms, and varying water depths for aquatic turtles. Give terrestrial turtles spaces to explore that have a variety of substrates and things.

Keeping an eye on and modifying enrichment

Evaluate the enrichment's efficacy on a regular basis and make any adjustments. Make sure the turtles are engaging with the enrichment and getting something out of it by keeping an eye on their behaviour. To keep enrichment items effective and the turtles interested, replace or alter them on a regular basis.

CHAPTER EIGHT

Daily Upkeep And Repair

Standard Cleaning Techniques

In a farming setting, the health and welfare of turtles depend on proper daily care and upkeep. Regular cleaning is one of the most important parts of this maintenance. The best living circumstances are maintained, sickness is prevented, and trash is managed when the turtle habitat is cleaned on a regular basis.

1. Cleaning of Habitats

Take a close look at the turtle's habitat first. Look for any indications of mould growth or garbage accumulation. Clear the enclosure of any food scraps, faeces, and debris. To remove solid waste from the water, use a net or scoop. If the substrate gets soiled, rinse it.

To keep the water in enclosures with a water feature fresh, replenish some of the water every day. Verify the water filtration system's proper operation and clean it in accordance with the manufacturer's recommendations. This contributes to preserving the purity of the water and lowering dangerous germs.

2. Sanitisation of the Surface

Once visible garbage has been removed, sanitise surfaces to get rid of bacteria and algae. Employ cleaning supplies that are safe for turtles and non-toxic. Strong chemicals like bleach should be avoided as they may hurt the turtles. Instead, use gentle detergents and be sure to rinse any cleaned surfaces well to get rid of any leftover cleaner.

3. Cleaning of Accessories and Equipment

Make sure all accessories, including feeding bowls, hiding places, and basking platforms, are clean. Use a brush to give them a thorough scrub, then make sure all the residue is gone by rinsing well. Cleaning these things on a regular basis keeps bacteria from growing and guarantees the turtles' safety and comfort.

4. Schedule of Regular Maintenance

Create a cleaning plan that works with your farming setup and the requirements of your species of turtles.

Removing waste and spot-checking the water quality are examples of daily cleaning duties. Deeper cleaning of the habitat and its accessories may be necessary every other or every week. To maintain consistency and keep track of these chores, keep a cleaning journal.

Keeping An Eye On Turtle Behaviour

It is essential to watch turtle behaviour to spot any changes in health or wellbeing. Frequent monitoring enables prompt action by assisting in the early detection of symptoms of sickness or discomfort.

1. Observations of Behaviour

Every day, take some time to observe the turtles as they navigate their surroundings. Keep an eye out for any changes in their social interactions with other turtles, eating patterns, and activity levels. In general, healthy turtles are energetic and display their regular activities, like swimming, basking, and foraging.

2. Indicators of Health

Keep an eye out for any indications of disease or anxiety. Unusual hostility, appetite loss, or tiredness are examples of behavioural changes that may point to health problems. Physical indicators such as irregularities in the shell, pigmentation changes, or discharge from the eyes should be observed. Frequent examinations can aid in the early detection of problems and offer the chance for quick treatment.

3. Social Exchanges

Watch the interactions between turtles. In small areas, hostile behaviour or dominance problems can occasionally arise. Make sure every turtle has enough room and supplies to reduce strain and rivalry. Aggressive encounters might require habitat modifications or individual isolation.

4. Adaptation to Environment

Keep an eye on how turtles adjust to their surroundings. Their behaviour may be impacted by modifications to the illumination, temperature, or habitat design. Make sure that the environmental factors, including the temperature of the water and the locations for basking, are ideal for the particular kind of turtle you are raising.

Maintaining And Managing Records

Maintaining accurate records is essential to running a turtle farm. Thorough documentation facilitates the monitoring of the turtles' well-being, conduct, and general supervision, guaranteeing that every facet of their upkeep is attended to.

1. Medical Records

Keep thorough medical records for every turtle. Keep records of all vaccines, treatments, and regular health examinations. Note any symptoms of disease, wounds, or strange conduct. This data facilitates the tracking of each turtle's medical history and assists with disease diagnosis and treatment.

2. Logs of Behaviour

Note all the behaviours you see, such as eating patterns, social interactions, and variations in activity levels. This record can offer insightful information about the turtles' welfare and assist in spotting any trends or problems that might need to be addressed.

3. surroundings

Keep track of environmental data, like lighting, pH levels, and water temperature. The habitat is kept within the optimal range for the health of the turtles through routine observation and documentation of these variables

If any parameters are not within the recommended range, they can be quickly adjusted.

4. Inventory Control

Keep a record of the supplies' inventory, which should include food, cleaning supplies, and equipment. Keep an eye on your inventory to make sure you have enough supplies for routine upkeep and care. Planning ahead and creating a budget are made easier with effective inventory management.

5. Procedure Documentation

Keep a record of every cleaning and maintenance operation. Provide specifics regarding the tasks' frequency, the techniques employed, and any observations made. This paperwork acts as a guide for constant upkeep and offers a foundation for assessing how well your maintenance schedule is working.

CHAPITRE NINE

Promoting And Getting Rid Of Turtles

Recognising The Market

Overview of the Market Dynamics for Turtle Farming

Within the larger aquaculture sector, turtle farming is a specialised but growing industry. Recognising the different elements impacting consumer preferences,

market trends, and demand is essential to understanding the market. The market dynamics of each of the numerous segments that comprise turtle farming are distinct, such as food goods, pets, and ornamental turtles. Understanding these markets and the demands they have is essential to marketing and selling turtles successfully.

Target Audience and Market Segmentation

Based on their intended uses, turtles can be divided into three main markets: pets, food, and conservation. The purchase habits and client profiles of each group vary. For example, whereas food markets emphasise the culinary characteristics and sustainability of turtles, pet buyers look for turtles that are easy to care for and have an attractive appearance. For study or reintroduction into the wild, turtle farming may be of interest to environmentalists. Recognising and comprehending these markets enables marketing plans to be adapted to the unique requirements of target audiences.

The Currents Affecting Turtle Farming

The turtle farming sector is being shaped by a number of developments. Demand has been spurred by growing interest in exotic pets and environmentally friendly feeding sources. A rise in interest in farmed turtles has also been attributed to growing knowledge of conservation and the effects of wild harvesting on turtle populations. Keeping up with these trends will help you better understand customer preferences and match your marketing initiatives with what the market is now demanding.

Comparative Evaluation

If you want to position your turtle farming firm efficiently, you must analyse your competition. Examine the products, pricing policies, and marketing techniques of other turtle farms and companies operating in your area or speciality. Knowing their advantages and disadvantages will enable you to spot areas where you may stand out from the competition and provide superior value or unique selling propositions.

A Legal and Ethical Perspective

There are several laws and moral issues with the turtle farming business. It is crucial to comprehend and abide by all applicable laws regarding turtle farming, including those pertaining to permits, environmental restrictions, and animal welfare standards. A positive brand reputation and market acceptance are also significantly influenced by ethical practices in turtle farming, such as humane treatment and sustainable breeding techniques.

Strategies For Pricing

Factors Affecting the Price

A number of elements need to be taken into account while determining the appropriate price for your turtles, such as competition pricing, market demand, and production expenses. To establish a base price, add up all of the production costs (feed, labour, healthcare, and infrastructure). Pricing is also influenced by the dynamics of supply and demand in the market; low supply or strong demand might support higher prices, while an excess of supply may call for competitive pricing.

Pricing models and cost analysis

To find the cost per turtle, including both fixed and variable costs, do a thorough cost analysis. Select a pricing strategy based on this study that supports your company's objectives. Cost-plus pricing, in which a markup is applied to the cost of production, and value-based pricing, in which the price is determined by the customer's perceived value, are examples of common pricing methods. Make sure the model you've selected generates a respectable profit margin and covers costs.

Competitive Rates

Make sure your price is both lucrative and competitive by researching the pricing tactics used by your rivals. While maintaining a competitive edge is crucial, underpricing should be avoided as this may result in a reduced perceived value and possible financial hardship. Rather, concentrate on providing distinctive value propositions to support your pricing, such better quality, outstanding customer service, or extra advantages.

Pricing Techniques for Various Market Groups

Pricing methods may differ depending on the market niche. For example, the rarity and visual appeal of decorative turtles may drive up the cost, but the size and quality of food turtles may determine the price. Adjust your pricing based on the unique needs and willingness to pay of each market segment.

Discounts & Promotional Prices

Use price techniques that are promotional to draw clients and increase revenue. Seasonal promotions, package deals, and time-limited discounts can increase demand and boost sales. Make sure, though, that promotional pricing does not interfere with profitability and is consistent with your entire price plan.

Channels Of Sales And Customer Engagement

Finding the Sales Channels

Reaching your target audience and increasing revenue require effective sales channels. Turtle farming commonly uses partnerships with pet stores or restaurants, direct sales through farm visits or internet platforms, and participation in trade exhibits or expos as sales channels. Select the channels that best fit your target market and business style, as each has benefits and drawbacks.

Establishing a Virtual Identity

In the current digital era, reaching a wider audience requires having a strong online presence. Make a polished website that features your turtles, tells visitors about your farming methods, and provides simple ways to make purchases. Make use of social media channels to interact with prospective clients, post updates, and create a brand community.

Partnerships and Networking

Establishing strategic alliances with eateries, pet retailers, or environmental advocacy groups can expand your market penetration. Work together to provide your turtles to their clients or include them into their products. Networking inside the sector might also yield insightful information and expansion prospects.

Reaching Out to and Engaging with Customers

Actively interacting with both current and potential consumers is essential to effective customer outreach. To foster relationships and get feedback, put tactics like email marketing, consumer surveys, and loyalty programs into practice. Excellent customer service and tailored communication may build trust and promote repeat business.

Keeping an eye on and modifying sales strategies

Keep an eye on the success of your sales tactics and make any adjustments. To make well-informed decisions, monitor sales performance, examine client feedback, and keep abreast with industry developments. Maintaining competitiveness and satisfying changing client needs requires response and flexibility.

Through a comprehensive market analysis, strategic pricing, and efficient sales channels, you may effectively market and sell turtles, setting up your farm for expansion and success in this distinct sector of the economy.

Chapter Ten

A Legal And Ethical Perspective

Rules And Adherence

Recognising State and Federal Laws

It's imperative that you become informed with the local and federal laws regulating turtle farming before beginning a business. Many laws aimed at safeguarding the animals and their environments apply to turtle farming. The kinds of turtles that can be farmed, the circumstances in which they must be housed, and the licenses needed to do so lawfully may vary depending on the area.

Zoning ordinances that specify the locations of turtle farms are frequently part of local regulations. Broader topics like trade restrictions and wildlife preservation may be covered by national rules. For example, rules in many nations forbid cultivating endangered animals or need for certain permits to be obtained in order to care for them. Knowing these laws can help you make sure your farm stays within the law and supports conservation efforts rather than undermines them.

Licenses and Permit Requirements

Obtaining different licenses and permits is typically necessary to start a turtle farm. These may include licenses for businesses, permits for hunting, and even permissions for particular types of agriculture. Keeping and raising turtles requires a wildlife permit, particularly when dealing with protected species. The application procedure for these permits can be difficult and time-consuming, requiring thorough documentation of your facilities, farming methods, and strategies for protecting the turtles' welfare.

Any commercial endeavour that wants to operate needs a business licence. Agricultural permits may also be necessary if your turtle farming affects the surrounding environment or requires a large amount of land. You may steer clear of legal problems and fines by making sure you have all the necessary permits before you begin.

Observance of International Treaties

You have to abide by international treaties and accords if your turtle farming operation involves commerce with other countries. One such agreement that governs the worldwide trading of threatened and endangered species, including several species of turtles, is the Convention on worldwide trading in Endangered Species of Wild Fauna and Flora (CITES). Adhering to CITES regulations guarantees that your activities do not exacerbate the natural fall in turtle populations.

Other international accords, in addition to CITES, can also be applicable based on your region and the species you are farming. It is crucial to comprehend these agreements in order to make sure that your farming methods comply with international conservation initiatives and trade laws.

Ethical Methods In Agriculture
Enhancing the Well-Being of Animals

Animal welfare is given first priority in ethical turtle farming procedures. This entails supplying suitable living quarters, guaranteeing a healthy diet, and quickly attending to medical concerns. For them to flourish, environments with certain temperature ranges, humidity levels, and enough room to roam around and behave naturally are necessary. Maintaining these circumstances promotes the turtles' general wellbeing by reducing stress and health issues.

Moreover, routine veterinarian care is essential. Turtles should be kept an eye out for any indications of disease or harm, and when necessary, fast medical care should be given. Farmers that practise ethics make sure that their animals are given the finest care and don't have to suffer needlessly.

Conservation and Breeding

The focus of ethical turtle farming methods is frequently on breeding initiatives that support turtle species conservation. Conscious farmers encourage turtle breeding in ways that improve the population's genetic variety and general health.

Programs for selective breeding that aim to enhance genetic features and lower the likelihood of inherited illnesses may be a part of this.

Ethical turtle farms might engage in habitat restoration and educational initiatives in addition to raising turtles. Farmers may make sure that their operations have a beneficial effect on turtle numbers and their natural habitats by supporting conservation programs.

Steer clear of exploitative tactics

Overbreeding and employing turtles for non-essential purposes are examples of exploitative activities that are avoided in ethical turtle husbandry. Profit should never come before the welfare of the animals for farmers. Activities like overcrowding or subpar living circumstances that put turtles through unnecessary stress or injury are regarded as unethical.

Moreover, ethical farming calls for openness and truthfulness in sales and marketing. This entails informing prospective purchasers of the turtles' origins and current state in a clear and understandable manner and making sure that all statements made regarding the animals' well-being and calibre are true.

Impact On The Environment
Evaluating and Reducing the Impact on the Environment

Both beneficial and negative effects on the ecosystem might result from turtle farming. An essential component of ethical farming techniques is recognising and reducing these impacts. Waste product contamination is a major environmental concern because it can have an impact on nearby water supplies and ecosystems.

Putting in place efficient waste management systems is essential to cutting pollution. In order to prevent pollution of the surrounding areas, this may entail managing solid waste and employing filtering devices to purify water before it is released into the environment. Turtle farms should also make an effort to run their operations using eco-friendly products and procedures.

Preservation of Habitat

Making sure farming operations don't damage natural ecosystems is a crucial part of minimising environmental effect.

This entails preventing land degradation or deforestation, which may happen if the farm grows larger. It is important to use sustainable land management techniques to save the nearby ecosystems.

In order to mitigate any detrimental effects, farmers might also work on habitat restoration projects. This could include reclaiming wetlands, planting native plants, or funding regional conservation efforts. Turtle farmers can support environmental conservation by actively preserving and restoring their natural habitats.

Use of Sustainable Resources

For turtle farming, resource sustainability is a major factor. This involves making efficient use of resources including energy, feed, and water. One way to lessen the farm's total environmental impact is to deploy energy-efficient technologies and water recycling systems.

It is imperative for farmers to take sustainability of the turtle feed into account. A key component of moral and sustainable agricultural methods is selecting feed sources that are kind to the environment and do not deplete natural resources.

CHAPTER ELEVEN

Developing And Growing Your Farm

Careful planning and execution are necessary when growing and scaling a turtle farming business. Your farm's infrastructure, personnel, and financial plan will need to change as the demand for your turtles increases in order to maintain profitability. The main topics of scaling and growing your turtle farm are covered in this chapter, along with advice on hiring and training workers, building out your infrastructure, and making growth-related financial plans.

Developing Infrastructure

Evaluating the Requirements for Current Infrastructure

Assessing your present infrastructure is the first step towards scaling your turtle farm successfully. Determine how big your current breeding spaces, filtration systems, and tanks can hold. Assess whether the additional turtles can be housed in your current configuration or if improvements are required. Take into account the following components:

• Tank Capacity and Design: Determine whether the extra load can be handled by your current tanks. Turtles may require larger or more tanks in order to have enough room for growth and development.

• Water Filtration and Quality Systems: As you have additional turtles, you will need to upgrade your filtration and water quality systems. It could be necessary to upgrade to more energy-efficient systems or add more units in order to maintain ideal water conditions.

• Breeding and Nursery spaces: Determine if you have enough space in your breeding and nursery spaces to accommodate more hatchlings. Increasing the size or quality of these spaces can help with breeding initiatives.

Putting Money Into New Technologies

Investing in innovative technologies can improve your turtle farm's productivity and efficiency. Examine the following developments in technology:

• Automatic Feeding Systems: By lowering labour expenses and guaranteeing regular feeding schedules, automatic feeders can assist in the efficient management of large numbers of turtles.

• Advanced Monitoring Systems: By putting in place advanced monitoring systems, farmers may improve overall farm management by tracking temperature, water quality, and other important indicators in real-time.

• Energy-Efficient Equipment: To save operating expenses and lessen environmental effect, think about replacing your heating, cooling, and lighting systems with more energy-efficient models.

Planning for Expansion

Plan your infrastructure growth with future expansion in mind. Consider scalability by utilising modular layouts and designs. Important things to think about are:

• Modular Tank Systems: As your farm expands, modular tank systems make expansion simple. With this method, adding or rearranging tanks is possible without requiring extensive overhauls.

• Adaptable Facility Layouts: When designing a facility, keep future upgrades and changes in operational requirements in mind. As your farm grows, open plans and flexible areas can help make changes easier.

Employing And Educating Personnel
Determine Staffing Requirements

Your team will need to grow as your turtle farm expands in order to handle more operations.

Determine the precise responsibilities and abilities needed for efficient farm management:

• Aquatic professionals: Hiring qualified aquatic professionals guarantees that the water quality is kept at ideal levels and that your turtles receive the right care.

• Breeding Technicians: In overseeing hatchling development and administering breeding operations, breeding technicians are essential.

• Maintenance Workers: Managing infrastructure, such as tanks, filtration systems, and other equipment, requires maintenance workers.

Creating Instructional Plans

To make sure that your employees are capable of handling their obligations, you must implement effective training programs. Pay attention to the following:

- Standard Operating Procedures (SOPs): Create thorough SOPs for all aspects of everyday operations, including as cleaning, feeding, and controlling water quality. Make certain that every employee is conversant with these protocols.

- Technical Training: Offer instruction in the use of new apparatus, systems, and technologies. This training aids employees in maintaining high standards of care and adjusting to changes.

- Health and Safety Procedures: Train employees in health and safety to make sure they understand the proper ways to handle turtles, dispose of garbage, and have a safe workplace.

Creating a Positive Workplace Culture

Employee retention and performance can both be improved in a favourable work environment. Think about the following tactics:

- Clear Communication: Encourage open lines of communication between employees and management. Team chemistry can be enhanced and issues can be addressed via regular meetings and feedback sessions.

- Professional Development: Provide chances for career progression and professional growth. This can involve going to conferences and workshops, as well as getting further certificates.

- Acknowledgement and Rewards: Give employees credit for their accomplishments and contributions. This might inspire dedication to the farm's success and raise morale.

Planning Your Finances For Growth

Making a Budget for Growth

Creating a thorough budget is crucial to handling the monetary side of expanding your turtle farm. Think about the following elements:

- Infrastructure Costs: Determine how much building, equipment, and technological investments will cost while increasing your infrastructure. Put money aside in your budget for these kinds of costs.

- Staffing Costs: These comprise pay, benefits, and the cost of onboarding new employees' training. Take into account prospective pay raises as well as other personnel-related expenses.

- Operational Expenses: Set aside money for escalating expenses related to upkeep, feed, and utilities. Keep a tight eye on these costs to make sure they match your budgetary estimates.

Examining Available Funds

One of the most important things you can do to help your farm grow is to secure money. Examine the following sources of funding:

- Loans and Grants: Look into the loans and grants that are available to companies engaged in aquaculture or agriculture. These monetary resources can assist in funding growth efforts and defraying expansion costs.

- Investors: Take into account luring in backers who are eager to help your farm expand. To submit to possible investors, compile a thorough company plan and financial predictions.

- Crowdfunding: Platforms for crowdsourcing can be a good way to raise money. To draw supporters, create an engaging campaign that emphasises the goals and expansion possibilities of your farm.

Keeping an Eye on Financial Performance

To make sure your expansion plans are on track, keep a close eye on your financial performance. Important procedures consist of:

- Financial Reporting: To monitor revenue, costs, and profitability, put in place a reliable financial reporting system. Examine financial statements on a regular basis and contrast them with your predictions and budget.

- Performance indicators: Determine the most important performance indicators to evaluate the efficacy and efficiency of your growth initiatives. Return on investment, cost per turtle, and revenue growth are a few examples of metrics that might offer insightful data.

- Modifying Strategies: Be ready to modify your financial plans in light of performance information. If you run into difficulties or inconsistencies, adjust as needed to keep on course.

Your turtle farm will need to be scaled up and expanded with careful planning and strategic execution. You may successfully manage development and guarantee the long-term viability of your farm by concentrating on infrastructure expansion, staffing, and financial planning.

Conclusin

For anyone interested in learning more about sustainable agriculture and animal conservation, turtle farming is an exciting and unique opportunity. This chapter will cover the essential elements of establishing and running a turtle farm, emphasising the value of careful planning, dedication, and ongoing education.

Considering the Important Lessons

Selecting the proper species and establishing a suitable habitat are just two of the many factors to take into account when starting a turtle farm. For the sake of the health and productivity of various turtle species, whether they are aquatic or terrestrial, it is essential to comprehend their unique requirements. For example, while terrestrial turtles require a safe and suitable environment on land, aquatic turtles require well-maintained water conditions and a balanced diet.

One important thing to remember is how important careful planning is. Detailed study and a well-defined business plan are the first steps towards a prosperous turtle farm. The goals of the farm, including whether it is being operated for commercial, conservation, or a combination of both, should be described in this plan. It should also include the moral and legal issues related to turtle farming, making sure that regional laws and global norms are followed.

Problems and Solutions

A number of difficulties could come up during the process, such as problems with disease control, habitat upkeep, and market swings. Diseases that affect turtle health and farm productivity include respiratory infections and shell rot. It is imperative to put preventive measures into practice, such as routine health examinations and upholding ideal living conditions.

Another crucial aspect is habitat maintenance. To stop the spread of illness and to make sure the turtles are healthy, a clean and secure environment must be provided. A successful farming operation relies on essential principles such as effective waste management, regular cleaning schedules, and water quality monitoring.

The Prospects for Turtle Farming

In the long run, turtle farming offers chances for development and innovation. Research and technological developments can result in more effective breeding methods, better farming techniques, and better health management. Long-term success will depend on how well we embrace these developments while staying dedicated to moral and sustainable business practices.

The future of turtle farming also entails raising public awareness and educating the public about the advantages of sustainable agricultural methods and turtle protection. Turtle farmers can encourage others to pursue this fulfilling career by contributing to larger conservation initiatives and exchanging knowledge and experiences.

To sum up, novice turtle farmers need to have a combination of enthusiasm, expertise, and commitment. Beginners can establish a profitable and morally-responsible turtle farming business by being aware of industry trends, anticipating problems, and comprehending the unique demands of turtles. Although the trek may be difficult, it is beneficial because it will help save species and promote sustainable practices.

THE END

www.ingramcontent.com/pod-product-compliance
Lightning Source LLC
Chambersburg PA
CBHW070955240526
45469CB00016B/1136